T0159894

 Published by Ice House Books

JOLLY AWESOME is the design studio of London-based illustrator Matt Nguyen.
His collections are inspired by his love of Americana, British pop-culture and stuff that makes him smile.

Illustrated by JOLLY AWESOME
Designed by Joe Peter Brown

p6 mirzamik / shutterstock.com
p9 Brent Hofacker / shutterstock.com
p11 vsl / shutterstock.com
p13 TalyaAL / shutterstock.com
p15 jose m feito / shutterstock.com
p17 Alp Aksoy / shutterstock.com
p19 Evgeny Karandaev / shutterstock.com
p21 Shyripa Alexandr / shutterstock.com
p23 Sea Wave / shutterstock.com
p25 Goskova Tatiana / shutterstock.com
p27 Sunny Forest / shutterstock.com
p29 Andreas Argirakis / shutterstock.com
p31 Vjacheslav Shishlov / shutterstock.com
p33 Andrei Mayatnik / shutterstock.com

p35 Evgeny Karandaev / shutterstock.com
p37 Elena Lapshina / shutterstock.com
p39 Irina Rostokina / shutterstock.com
p41 Brent Hofacker / shutterstock.com
p43 Andrei Mayatnik / shutterstock.com
p45 Shyripa Alexandr / shutterstock.com
p47 Alp Aksoy / shutterstock.com
p49 Brent Hofacker / shutterstock.com
p51 Brent Hofacker / shutterstock.com
p53 Alp Aksoy / shutterstock.com
p55 Brent Hofacker / shutterstock.com
p57 Alfa Photostudio / shutterstock.com
p59 Nitr / shutterstock.com
p61 Zadorozhna Natalia / shutterstock.com

Ice House Books is an imprint of Half Moon Bay Limited
The Ice House, 124 Walcot Street, Bath, BA1 5BG
www.halfmoonbay.co.uk

Please drink responsibly.

ISBN 978-1-912867-03-5

Printed in China

JOLLY AWESOME

LET THE FUN BE GIN!

GIN!

ICE HOUSE BOOKS

HOW TO MAKE...
SUGAR SYRUP

INGREDIENTS

240 ml (8.4 fl oz) water
200 g (7 oz) caster sugar

METHOD

1. Mix the sugar and water in a medium-sized saucepan.

2. Bring the mixture to the boil, constantly stirring until the sugar has fully dissolved and the liquid has thickened.

3. Allow the sugar syrup to cool completely, then transfer it to a glass container and keep in the fridge for up to one month.

CONTENTS

AN APPLE A DAY
(APPLE TEA COCKTAIL)

INGREDIENTS
(SERVES 2)

225 ml (7.9 fl oz) water
4 tsps honey
2 shots apple juice
3 apple slices
1 cinnamon stick
2 cloves
1 black tea bag
4 shots gin
1 shot Martini® Bianco
2 shots lemon juice

METHOD

1. In a large pot, add the water, honey, apple juice, apple slices, cinnamon stick and cloves. Slowly bring to a boil.

2. Take off the heat and add the black tea bag. Allow to brew for three minutes, then remove the tea bag, spices and apple.

3. Add the gin, Martini® Bianco and lemon juice. Turn the heat back on low and stir the mixture whilst warming for around 30 seconds.

4. Strain the mixture into two cups and garnish with apple or lemon slices.

IT REALLY IS THE BEE'S KNEES!

(BEE'S KNEES)

METHOD

2 shots gin
1 shot honey syrup
½ shot lemon juice
Mint leaf to serve

1. Fill a cocktail shaker with ice and add all the ingredients.

2. Shake until completely mixed and strain into a chilled cocktail glass. Garnish with a mint leaf and serve.

SO CHILLED

BERRY DELICIOUS BRAMBLE

(BLACKBERRY BRAMBLE)

INGREDIENTS
(SERVES 1)

Lemon slice & sugar to serve
6 blackberries
1 shot lemon juice
½ shot crème de cassis
½ shot sugar syrup
2 shots gin
Orange twist, cinnamon stick
& blackberries to garnish

METHOD

1. First, run a slice of lemon around the rim of your cocktail glass and dip the rim in sugar.

2. Add the blackberries to the glass and crush them with a muddler. Add the lemon juice and fill the glass with ice.

3. In a cocktail shaker, stir together the crème de cassis, sugar syrup and gin, then add to your glass.

4. Stir to combine the ingredients, then garnish with orange twists, cinnamon and blackberries.

DON'T CRY OVER SPILT MILK. IT COULD'VE BEEN GIN.

(BLUEBERRY GIN DAISY)

INGREDIENTS
(SERVES 1)

2 shots gin
1 shot lemon juice
½ shot blueberry grenadine
Tonic water
Lime zest to garnish
Sliced cucumber to garnish

METHOD

1. Shake the gin, lemon juice and blueberry grenadine in an ice-filled cocktail shaker until the outside of the shaker gets cold.

2. Strain into an ice-filled glass and top with tonic water. Garnish with a lime twist and slice of cucumber on the rim.

CUCUMBER IN MY GIN IS ONE OF MY FIVE A DAY

(CUCUMBER GIN SPRITZ)

INGREDIENTS
(SERVES 4)

1 cucumber
4 shots gin
2 shots sugar syrup
4 glasses Prosecco
A little tonic water
Rosemary sprigs to garnish

METHOD

1. Use a vegetable peeler to cut 12 long strips of cucumber. Set aside.

2. Cut the leftover cucumber into small chunks and pulp it with ice in a cocktail shaker.

3. Add the gin and sugar syrup to the shaker, then shake together for around 30 seconds.

4. Strain the cocktail into four glasses and top each glass with Prosecco and a little tonic water. Stir the cocktails and add cucumber ribbons and a sprig of rosemary.

I'M
FRESH
AF!

VERY DIRTY MARTINI

(DIRTY MARTINI)

INGREDIENTS
(SERVES 1)

2 shots gin
½ shot dry vermouth
Olive oil to taste
Olives to garnish

METHOD

1. Place cubes of ice in a martini glass to chill it.

2. Put the gin and dry vermouth in a separate mixing glass and add a drop of olive oil (according to personal taste).

3. Remove the ice from the martini glass and strain the cockatil into the chilled glass. Garnish with two olives on a cocktail stick.

WHEN LIFE GIVES YOU ORANGES
(ORANGE & LIME MULE)

INGREDIENTS
(SERVES 1)

2 shots gin
1 shot lime juice
1 shot orange juice
1 shot ginger beer
Orange slice to garnish
Mint to garnish

METHOD

1. Pour the gin, fruit juices and ginger beer into an ice-filled glass and stir until well mixed.

2. Garnish with a slice of orange and sprig of mint.

GRAPE-FUL FOR GIN

(GIN & ELDERFLOWER GREYHOUND)

INGREDIENTS
(SERVES 1)

Grapefruit slices
Rosemary sprigs
3 shots gin
½ shot elderflower liqueur
Dash of tonic water
Grapefruit juice to top up glass

METHOD

1. Put ice cubes, grapefruit slices and rosemary sprigs in a glass.

2. Add the gin, elderflower liqueur and dash of tonic, then top up the glass with grapefruit juice. Stir gently to combine.

SO HOT RIGHT NOW
(GIN MINT HOT CHOCOLATE)

INGREDIENTS
(SERVES 1)

2 shots double cream
1 tsp icing sugar
Peppermint extract
3 shots whole milk
50 g (1.8 oz) dark chocolate
1 shot crème de menthe
1 shot gin

METHOD

1. In a small bowl, whip the double cream. Add the icing sugar and a couple of drops of peppermint extract, and stir until combined. Leave in the fridge to chill while you do the next steps.

2. Add the milk to a large saucepan and simmer on a medium heat, stirring regularly. When the milk is hot (not boiling), take it off the heat and stir in the dark chocolate (chopped) until it has completely melted. Return to the heat, add the crème de menthe and gin, and stir to combine.

3. Pour the hot drink into a tall latte glass. Finish with a dollop of the whipped cream and grate some dark chocolate on top.

NECK IT
(LONG ISLAND ICED TEA)

INGREDIENTS
(SERVES 1)

Lime slices
½ shot gin
½ shot vodka
½ shot tequila
½ shot white rum
½ shot triple sec
1 shot lemon juice
1 shot sugar syrup
⅓ can of fizzy cola

METHOD

1. Fill a tall glass with ice and slices of lime.

2. In an ice-filled cocktail shaker, add the spirits, lemon juice and sugar syrup. Shake well.

3. Strain the mixture into the ice-filled glass and top with fizzy cola.

I'M ABSOLUTELY SHIT-FACED.

SAVE WATER: DRINK GIN
(MONKEY GLAND)

INGREDIENTS
(SERVES 1)

2 shots gin
1 shot fresh orange juice
½ shot grenadine
Dash of absinthe

METHOD

1. Run a dash of absinthe around the inside of a cocktail glass and pour away the excess.

2. In an ice-filled cocktail shaker, add the gin, orange juice and grenadine. Shake well and strain into the cocktail glass. Then serve!

GIN-GLE BELLS
(MULLED GIN)

INGREDIENTS
(SERVES 1)

2 shots gin
2 shots apple juice
2 tbsps honey
Cloves
Orange slice to garnish

METHOD

1. In a large pan on a medium heat, stir together the gin, apple juice, honey and cloves until warm. Do not allow to boil.

2. Strain into a chunky glass or mug, and serve with a slice of orange on the rim.

I'LL REGRET THIS
(NAPOLEON)

INGREDIENTS
(SERVES 1)

2 shots gin
1 shot orange liqueur
½ shot red vermouth
Orange slice to garnish

1. In an ice-filled cocktail shaker, add the gin, liqueur and vermouth and shake well.

2. Strain the mixture into a chilled cocktail glass and add a slice of orange to serve.

GIN IS THE ANSWER. WHAT WAS THE QUESTION?
(NEGRONI)

INGREDIENTS
(SERVES 1)

1½ shots gin
1½ shots vermouth
1 shot Campari®
Orange slices to garnish

METHOD

1. Fill a mixing glass or cocktail shaker with ice and stir in the gin, vermouth and Campari® for 30 seconds (do not shake).

2. Strain into a cocktail glass over ice and garnish with slices of orange.

THIS IS
LEGINDARY

OH, AREN'T YOU SWEET?
(PARMA VIOLET COCKTAIL)

INGREDIENTS
(SERVES 1)

1½ shots vodka
1½ shots gin
½ shot crème de violette
Raspberries to garnish
Lavender sprigs to garnish

METHOD

1. In an ice-filled cocktail shaker, add the vodka, gin and crème de violette. Shake until the outside of the shaker gets cold.

2. Strain the mixture into a glass over ice. Add a couple of raspberries and a sprig of lavender to garnish.

I WANT IN!

A PINK FLAMINGO

(PINK FLAMINGO)

INGREDIENTS
(SERVES 1)

1½ shots vodka
1½ shots triple sec
Dash of sloe gin
Orange juice to top up glass
Orange slices to garnish
Rosemary sprig to garnish
Pomegranate seeds to garnish

METHOD

1. Fill a glass with ice and add the vodka, triple sec and sloe gin.

2. Top up the glass with orange juice and stir to mix all the ingredients.

3. Garnish with orange slices, a sprig of rosemary and pomegranate seeds.

INSTAGRAMMABLE AF

IT'S HEADING SOUTH

(SOUTHSIDE)

INGREDIENTS
(SERVES 1)

2 shots gin
1 shot lime juice
1 shot soda water
2 dashes grapefruit bitters
2 tsps sugar
Mint leaves to garnish
Cucumber ribbon to garnish

METHOD

1. In a tall glass, pour all the ingredients over ice and stir until the sugar is dissolved.

2. Garnish with mint leaves and a rolled cucumber ribbon.

TOM MADE ME DO IT
(TOM COLLINS)

INGREDIENTS
(SERVES 1)

2 shots gin
1 shot lemon juice
½ shot sugar syrup
Soda water
Lemon & cucumber to garnish

METHOD

1. Add a few ice cubes to a tall glass.

2. In an ice-filled cocktail shaker, add the gin, lemon juice and sugar syrup and shake well.

3. Strain the mixture into the glass and top up with soda water. Garnish with lemon and cucumber slices and a lemon twist.

TOO SEXY FOR
MY GLASS

I GO TO THE GIN EVERYDAY

(SINGAPORE SLING)

INGREDIENTS
(SERVES 1)

1 shot gin
1 shot cherry liqueur
1 shot Bénédictine®
1 shot lime juice
Soda water
Pineapple slice to garnish

METHOD

1. Chill a cocktail shaker with ice. Remove most of the ice and add the gin, cherry liqueur, Bénédictine® and lime juice. Stir well to mix and chill the ingredients.

2. Pour into a tall glass (ice too) and top with soda water. Add a slice of pineapple on the rim to garnish.

RHUBARB & CUSTARD? RHUBARB & GIN.
(RHUBARB COCKTAIL)

INGREDIENTS
(SERVES 1)

1 shot gin
1 shot lime juice
1 shot Aperol®
1 dash rhubarb bitters
Rhubarb stalk to garnish
Rosemary sprig to garnish

METHOD

1. In an ice-filled cocktail shaker, combine the gin, lime juice, Aperol® and bitters and shake until chilled.

2. Pour over ice into your glass, and garnish with (cleaned) rhubarb stalks and a sprig of rosemary.

LET THE EVENING BE GIN
(FRENCH 75)

METHOD

2 shots gin
1 shot lemon juice
1 shot sugar syrup
2 shots Champagne
Lemon twist to garnish

1. In an ice-filled cocktail shaker, add the gin, lemon juice and sugar syrup. Shake until fully chilled then strain into a Champagne flute.

2. Top up the glass with Champagne and garnish with a lemon twist.

STRONG WOMEN NEED STRONG DRINKS
(VESPER)

INGREDIENTS
(SERVES 1)

3 shots gin
1 shot vodka
½ shot dry vermouth
Lemon twist to garnish

METHOD

1. In an ice-filled cocktail shaker, combine the gin, vodka and vermouth. Shake until chilled.

2. Strain into a chilled cocktail glass and garnish with a lemon twist.

SHIT. THAT HURT.

IT'S GONNA TAKE OFF
(AVIATION)

INGREDIENTS
(SERVES 1)

2 shots gin
½ shot Maraschino liqueur
¼ shot crème de violette
1 shot lemon juice
Cherry to garnish

METHOD

1. In an ice-filled shaker add the gin, Maraschino liqueur, crème de violette and lemon juice. Shake well until fully chilled.

2. Strain into a cocktail glass and add a cherry to garnish.

THIS IS CHERRIFIC

STIRRED.
NOT SHAKEN.
(GIBSON)

INGREDIENTS
(SERVES 1)

3 shots gin
½ shot dry vermouth
Cocktail onions to garnish

METHOD

1. Pour the gin and dry vermouth into a mixing glass and stir together.

2. Strain into a chilled cocktail glass and garnish with cocktail onions on a stick.

FUN JUICE
(SPARKLING BEETROOT COCKTAIL)

INGREDIENTS
(SERVES 6)

200 g (7 oz) grated beetroot
200 g (7 oz) caster sugar
4 shots lemon juice
4 shots gin
6 shots Aperol®
1 bottle Prosecco
Beetroot leaves to garnish

METHOD

1. Put the grated beetroot, sugar and lemon juice in a large bowl and stir together. Cool in the fridge for around one hour, stirring occasionally to dissolve the sugar.

2. Once the sugar is dissolved, use a sieve to squeeze the liquid from the mixture into a bowl. Discard the pulp. Add the gin to the bowl and stir well.

3. Pour ½ shot of the beetroot syrup into each glass, then add one shot of Aperol® and top with Prosecco. Add a beetroot leaf to garnish.

CONTAINS CAFFEINE & UNICORN DUST
(GIN ICED TEA)

INGREDIENTS
(SERVES 1)

3 shots gin
3 shots Earl Grey tea (brewed & chilled)
2 tsps lemon juice
Mint sprig to garnish

METHOD

1. Put the gin, tea and lemon juice into a tall, ice-filled glass. Stir well.

2. Garnish with a sprig of mint and enjoy!

MIGHT BE COFFEE, MIGHT BE GIN.
(GIN & CHOCOLATE COFFEE)

INGREDIENTS
(SERVES 4)

3 shots espresso
3 tsps caster sugar
5 shots gin
3 shots crème de cacao
Dark chocolate shavings

METHOD

1. First, make your espresso shots. Then, in a small pan on a medium heat, combine the espresso with the sugar.

2. Add the gin and crème de cacao and warm until the cocktail is simmering, then remove from heat.

3. Serve warm in mugs, topped with shavings of dark chocolate.